Aisha the Great

by Aisha Doris

Illustrated by Rondi Kutz

Copyright © 2019 by Aisha Doris
Illustrated by Rondi Kutz
All rights reserved. No part of this publication may be reproduced, distributed, or transmitted in any form or by any means, including photocopying, recording, or other electronic or mechanical methods, without the prior written permission of the author, except in the case of brief quotations embodied in critical reviews and certain other noncommercial uses permitted by copyright law.

ISBN 978-1-970079-21-0

Printed in the United States of America

To Catherine, Joshua and Jonnel you are my superheroes.

Hi, My name is Aisha. I'm from Brooklyn and it's boring!

I am the middle of three sisters and I do not recommend being born second.

The middle is for peanut butter and jelly, cream cookies and marshmallows, not people.

Especially not people who wear glasses!
I started wearing glasses at 2 years old and they've been stuck on my face ever since.

If I only had one wish, it would be to be from someplace else!

There are so many other cool cities in the world. with fascinating languages and clothes.

I bet if I was from someplace else I would become the most interesting girl in the world! But where would I choose?

How About London!

I could meet the Queen and make her soldiers laugh, drink strawberry tea and eat scones.

We would say things like, "Tally ho!" and "Cheers!"

Being from London is clever but Tokyo would be even better! How about Japan?

There's so much to do in Japan! I can visit the seat of the emperor in the morning and climb Mount Fuji in the afternoon.

But wait, how about a Spanish speaking country?
They also have bright colors and yummy food.

Costa Rica, Spain, or Mexico!

Because the way I talk is boring.

My glasses are boring.

I'm nobody special.

I just don't fit in here.

But you are special and unique!

You are kind, funny...

...the maker of the world's best chocolate-apricot pancakes.

You always look for ways to help people.

And you are so smart.

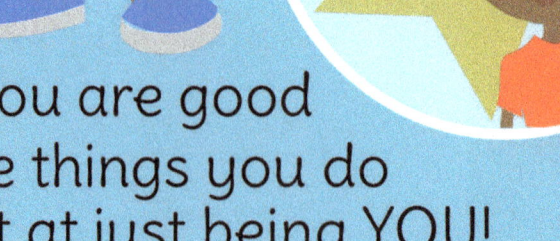

You are good at the things you do and great at just being YOU!

In fact, you are Aisha, the Great!
Doing great things for great people. You are perfect just the way you are and I love you.

And this super accessory will make you sparkle!

"Aisha, are you ready to go to the store?"

"Yes mom! I wonder who I can help today?"

www.ingramcontent.com/pod-product-compliance
Lightning Source LLC
Chambersburg PA
CBHW061116070526
44583CB00027B/3317